ANIMALS TO THE RESCUE!

///

AMAZING TRUE STORIES FROM AROUND THE WORLD

SANDRA MARKLE

M MILLBROOK PRESS | MINNEAPOLIS

FOR LIBRARY MEDIA SPECIALIST JILL MERKLE AND THE STUDENTS AT GREENSVIEW ELEMENTARY IN COLUMBUS, OHIO

The author would like to thank the following people for sharing their enthusiasm and expertise: Ian Fitzgibbon, Manager City Council, Warrnambool, Victoria, Australia; Dr. Jon Hanger, Australia Zoo Wildlife Warriors Worldwide, Beerwah, Queensland, Australia; Dr. Nan Hauser, Center for Cetacean Research and Conservation/Cook Islands Whale Research Project, Rarotonga, Cook Islands, South Pacific; Teresa MacPherson, FEMA Canine Work Group, Severna Park, Maryland; Fire Captain William Monahan, Los Angeles County Fire Department, Urban Search and Rescue, Fire Station 136, Palmdale, California; Lente Roode, Founder, Hoedspruit Endangered Species Centre, Hoedspruit, South Africa; Carolin Scheiter, IRO—Internationale Rettungshunde Organisation/International Search and Rescue Dog Organisation, Salzburg, Austria; Audrey Stone (Figo owner), Brewster, New York; Dr. Christopher Stremme, DVM, Faculty Syiah Kuala University, Banda Aceh, Indonesia; Roger Triantafilo, Castle Rock, Colorado; Dr. Anne Wallis, Deakin University, Warrnambool Campus, Victoria, Australia; Bart Weetjens, founder of APOPO, Krong Siem Reap, Cambodia; and David Williams, environmental scientist and conservation guardian dog trainer, Warrnambool, Victoria, Australia.

A special thank-you to Skip Jeffery for his loving support during the creative process.

Millbrook Press™
An imprint of Lerner Publishing Group, Inc.
241 First Avenue North
Minneapolis, MN 55401 USA

For reading levels and more information, look up this title at www.lernerbooks.com.

Designed by Mary Ross.
Main body text set in Myriad Pro.
Typeface provided by Adobe.

Library of Congress Cataloging-in-Publication Data

Names: Markle, Sandra, author.
Title: Animals to the rescue! : amazing true stories from around the world / Sandra Markle.
Description: Minneapolis : Millbrook Press , [2022] | Series: Sandra Markle's science discoveries | Includes bibliographical references and index. | Audience: Ages 8–14 | Audience: Grades 4–6 | Summary: "Did you know that rats can be heroes? So can a humpback whale! Discover incredible true stories about animals that have rescued humans—and other animals—in a book sure to appeal to animal lovers everywhere"— Provided by publisher.
Identifiers: LCCN 2020049136 (print) | LCCN 2020049137 (ebook) | ISBN 9781541581227 (library binding) | ISBN 9781728419077 (ebook)
Subjects: LCSH: Animal heroes—Anecdotes—Juvenile literature. | Animals—Anecdotes—Juvenile literature.
Classification: LCC QL791 .M344 2022 (print) | LCC QL791 (ebook) | DDC 590—dc23

LC record available at https://lccn.loc.gov/2020049136
LC ebook record available at https://lccn.loc.gov/2020049137

Manufactured in the United States of America
1-47321-47948-4/14/2021

CONTENTS

HERE COME THE HEROES!

Heroes come in all shapes and sizes. They're not just people who help others, like firefighters, teachers, and nurses. And they're not always *human*. No one knows when a natural disaster will strike or lives will be threatened. Sometimes in an emergency, an animal comes to the rescue. It may be an animal trained to use its special abilities to save people. Or it may be an animal responding courageously or doing what it naturally does, which happens to save a life. Sometimes animals even rescue other animals! Keep reading to discover the stories of some real-life animal heroes and the lives they saved.

This search and rescue dog is a key member of the South Korean Disaster Relief Team. Search teams came from many countries to help locate survivors after the January 12, 2010, earthquake that struck Port-au-Prince, Haiti.

WHALE OF A LIFEGUARD

September 2017
Rarotonga, Cook Islands

RAROTONGA,
COOK ISLANDS

DIVE TIME

On one September day in 2017, humpback whale researcher Nan Hauser was at work on her boat with her team in the South Pacific Ocean. The researchers were observing the humpback whales' behavior and snapping photos of their tails, creating a record of each whale they saw. July through October is the best time of year for observing humpback whales near the Cook Islands. That's when the whales pass the islands during their more than 4,000-mile (6,437 km) meandering migration from Antarctica, where they feast on small fish and shrimplike animals called krill, to warmer waters, where the females give birth and pairs mate.

However, one thing was different about Nan's daily research routine today. A film crew had come along to create a documentary about her work.

For more than twenty years, Nan Hauser has studied both the surface and underwater behavior of humpback whales.

Like human fingerprints, each humpback whale's tail flukes are unique. Scientists keep a photographic catalog to identify humpbacks by their tail shape and markings.

Humpback whales don't have teeth. Instead, they have baleen, rows of soft, bristlelike plates, that filter the shrimplike krill and other small food out of the seawater.

When they saw two large adult humpbacks, one of the filmmakers suggested Nan get into the water so they could capture a little more underwater footage of her swimming with the whales. Nan agreed and the film crew lowered the camera into the water. Then Nan slipped overboard, carrying her own waterproof video camera to take some closer footage of the whales. When she was some distance from the boat, the larger of the two humpbacks—which Nan guessed to be 50 feet (15 m) long and weighing many tons—turned and began surging through the water, heading straight for her.

As a longtime humpback researcher, Nan knew this was unusual behavior. Worse, she realized there wasn't time to swim out of the whale's way. Nan said, "I was afraid it was going to ram me."

Instead, the whale only bumped her. It pushed her back toward her boat. Nan was terrified of the whale's strength. But she forced herself to act calmly—even using the camera strapped to her hand to photograph the whale. Then the situation became much more serious. The humpback nudged her onto its chin and rolled her under its giant, armlike pectoral fin. Nan was trapped underwater, wearing only a snorkel and mask. She needed to reach the water's surface to breathe.

As usual, Nan Hauser had dived in wearing only a snorkel and mask. She had observed that the streaming bubbles from scuba gear upset the whales.

/// THE REST OF THE STORY

Somehow, Nan got out from under the whale's fin, surfaced, and sucked in a breath. But before she could swim away, the humpback tucked her under its fin again. Each time she escaped and took a breath, the whale would push her back underwater. She had no idea how long this went on. But, at last, she did get away from the whale.

Nan swam as fast as she could for her boat. Though her ordeal had only gone on for ten minutes, she was exhausted. She said, "Even as I heard my team shouting for me to swim faster, I felt myself slowing."

That was when the humpback whale caught up to Nan again. Only this time, it shoved her the short remaining distance to her boat, and her team hauled her aboard. It was only then, with everyone around her pointing, that Nan spotted the real danger in the water: a tiger shark. She said, "Tiger sharks are super aggressive and there was one—at least 15 feet [4.5 m] long—not far from the boat."

Nan realized the giant humpback whale hadn't been attacking her. It was protecting her from a possible shark attack. She believes she is the first person in recorded history to be rescued by a whale. This experience made Nan more determined than ever to work to protect humpback whales—in fact, all kinds of whales.

Scientists consider tiger sharks second only to great white sharks as being dangerous to humans because they're likely to attack swimmers.

Lammie to the Rescue

May 7, 2014
Hoedspruit, South Africa

HOEDSPRUIT, SOUTH AFRICA

SAFE BUT SAD

Rangers were patrolling the Kapama Private Game Reserve on May 7, 2014, when they heard an animal wailing. At 32,000 acres (12,950 ha), Kapama is one of South Africa's largest private game reserves, land set aside for animals to live safely. The rangers still had a lot of area to cover, but they took the time to track the sound.

What they discovered was a male southern white rhino calf next to its mother's body. The mother's horn had been chopped off, which meant poachers, or illegal hunters, had killed the female rhino. Even though the rangers had arrived too late to help the mother, they believed the calf, which looked to be about three months old, might survive. So they called Lente Roode.

The population of southern white rhinos is listed as Near Threatened by the International Union for Conservation of Nature (IUCN) Red List.

Lente directs the Hoedspruit Endangered Species Centre (HESC), which she founded on the Kapama Private Game Reserve. HESC's mission is to help rare, endangered animals—ones whose populations are so small they're at risk of becoming extinct, or having no living members. Lente said, "When the little rhino arrived, he was screaming. The poor thing was grieving for his mother."

No one could get the rhino calf that Lente named Gertjie (pronounced Gert-chee) to stop wailing. At his young age, Gertjie, or Little G as they nicknamed him, needed to eat every four hours. However, no matter how hard Lente and her team tried, nothing convinced Little G to drink the bottles of rhino milk formula. Lente said, "Orphaned rhinos can grieve to death, but I was determined to find a way to save this baby."

In 1986 Lente Roode and her family purchased the land that became Kapama Private Game Reserve. They planned to raise cattle. But, when they found themselves competing with wild predators and wild grazers, they decided protecting the wild animals was more important.

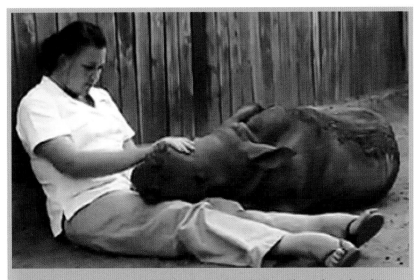

The team took turns staying around the clock with Little G, but he wouldn't be comforted—and he wouldn't eat.

/// NANNY NEEDED

Lente remembered seeing an ad in the local newspaper by a farmer selling Pedi sheep lambs. She knew Pedi sheep were strong defenders of their young, protecting them from predators. She wondered if such a feisty, four-legged companion might help Little G. Lente decided it was worth a try and purchased a lamb she named Lammie. When Lente put Lammie into Little G's pen, the baby rhino immediately stopped bawling. Lente was relieved. However, as soon as Little G finished looking Lammie over, he charged her.

Lente gasped, fearing for the lamb's life, but Lammie bounced out of Little G's way. And she kept on avoiding every attempt Little G made to butt her. When Little G finally stopped attacking, one of Lente's team leaned over the pen railing and held out a bottle of formula.

Mother southern white rhinos usually only give birth to one baby, born after developing for about sixteen months. The newborn is walking within a few hours.

Lammie mainly dined on alfalfa and grass, but she always licked Little G's meal buckets clean. And Little G sampled Lammie's food.

Lente said, "I was totally surprised—and delighted—when Little G trotted over and sucked the bottle dry."

From that wild introduction on, Little G and Lammie became inseparable. And the baby rhino never missed a meal again. Within a month, he was eating so much that he needed buckets full of formula for his meals. In between meals, he and Lammie went for walks, played chase, and took long naps together.

In the wild, a rhino calf nurses for one to two years and stays with its mother for protection for as long as three years.

/// THE REST OF THE STORY

Lammie proved to be a successful companion for Little G. So, when a newly orphaned rhino calf named Matimba arrived, Lente decided to try making the duo a trio. This time, though, when Matimba tried to butt Lammie, Little G charged to her defense. One head butt between the two rhinos was enough to end the fight and launch new friendships. A little later, Lente added two more young rhinos, Stompie and Balu, to what became known as Lammie's herd. Wherever Lammie went, the rhinos followed.

When the baby rhinos became teenagers, they were set free to roam wild on the surrounding land owned by Lente's family. There, rangers would always protect them from poachers. Lammie, on the other hand, stayed at the Hoedspruit Endangered Species Centre because she had a new job to do. An orphaned female elephant calf had arrived and wouldn't eat. That little calf really needed a four-legged friend—she needed Lammie.

These teenagers are on their way to becoming adult southern white rhinos. Then they'll weigh up to 6,000 pounds (2,722 kg) and stand up to 6 feet (1.8 m) tall at the shoulder.

THE RHINO CRISIS

A rhino's horn is really only useful to the rhino. The animal uses its horn to defend itself and its young and, sometimes, to dig for water. However, since ancient times, some people have believed rumors that a drink made of powdered rhino horn mixed with water is a medicine able to treat fevers, rheumatism, and even cancer. No scientific study has ever proven this. Still, the rumors have led some people to pay a lot of money for rhino horns, putting wild rhinos at risk of attack to collect their horns.

A rhino horn is like a human fingernail. It can easily be cut off and then grow back again. But since capturing the rhino takes time, poachers shoot to kill the rhinos in order to quickly cut off their horns. Or, worse, poachers sometimes shoot a dart at a rhino with medicine to quickly put it to sleep, rather than risk only wounding it and letting it escape. Then the poachers hack off the horns, leaving the animal with serious—even fatal—head wounds. Any baby rhinos such attacks leave orphaned are also likely to die— unless they are found and get help.

Compare this southern white rhino calf's horn to its mother's. For their first six months, rhino calves only have bumps where their horns will grow.

15

HeroRATs

September 17, 2015
Mozambique, Africa

HeroRAT handler Moses works with Rataplan, his land mine–sniffing rat.

SAFE AT LAST!

Mozambique once had among the world's largest number of buried land mines. These containers full of explosive material can blow up when stepped on or if a trip wire is pulled. During wars, land mines are buried along walking paths or in fields. Those land mines stay hidden after wars, and cause death and serious injuries long after the fighting stops.

More than 170,000 land mines were buried during Mozambique's fight for independence from Portugal and during the nearly twenty-year civil war that followed. Yet on September 17, 2015, the government of Mozambique announced the country was land mine-free. That was made possible with the help of African giant pouched rats trained to find the land mines. The rats were so light that they didn't trigger explosions, and their keen sense of smell helped them find where land mines were buried. This enabled specially equipped mine-removal teams to dig up and disable the explosive devices.

Training the rats to find land mines was Dutch product designer Bart Weetjens's idea. In his travels, he observed the terrible problem land mines caused, killing thousands of people each year and leaving many more permanently injured. He began exploring possible ways to locate buried land mines so they could be removed. When he read an article about gerbils being trained to detect scents, he remembered a pet rat he'd had as a boy. He discussed the possibility of training rats to sniff out land mines with rodent expert Ron Verhagen at the University of Antwerp. Verhagen thought it was a good idea and suggested trying to use the hardy, long-lived African giant pouched rat.

In 1997 Bart founded APOPO (initials for the Dutch name of the group, which in English means Anti-Personnel Landmines Detection Product Development) and ordered thirty wild African giant pouched rats to be delivered for training. Bart said, "I once saw one [of those rats] on a leash and figured they were easily tamed."

However, Bart got a big surprise when those first rats arrived at APOPO's warehouse training center in Antwerp, Belgium. The wild rats were fierce, attacking and biting one

Bart Weetjens went to Africa from Belgium because he wanted to work on a real-world problem, and he found one—land mines.

another and anyone who came close to them. It took Bart months of observing their behavior, especially at night when they were most active, before he realized keeping them together in one large pen was the mistake. So, he added partial walls to let the rats claim territories. But the real breakthrough happened when one female gave birth to pups and Bart was able to tame a young female. He named her Onzo, after a village in Angola that had many land mines. When seven-month-old Onzo gave birth to her first pups, Bart found that the pups were amazingly easy to tame. These rats became APOPO's first mine-detecting trainees, which Bart named the HeroRATs.

MEET THE HERORATS

African giant pouched rats are about the size of a small house cat. They are up to 17 inches (43 cm) long with an 18-inch-long (46 cm) hairless tail, and weigh up to 6 pounds (2.7 kg). That makes them light enough to walk safely over buried land mines, which usually require about 11 pounds (5 kg) of pressure to trigger an explosion.

African giant pouched rats are known for their keen sense of smell too. Once trained to detect TNT (the explosive material in land mines), the rats can smell it buried up to 8 inches (20 cm) deep and from about 3.2 feet (1 m) away.

Look at this African giant pouched rat's big cheeks. The rat has stuffed them full of food to carry away and bury for later when it's hungry again.

Land Mines Are a Terrible Problem

Explosive land mines were first used during the American Civil War (1861–1865) to kill or injure advancing troops. Since then, land mines have become weapons used in many conflicts around the world.

The African country of Angola is considered to be the country with the most land mines, but other countries with a high land mine risk include Egypt, Afghanistan, Bosnia-Herzegovina, Cambodia, Iraq, and Colombia. Despite a 1997 global ban on using these weapons, many land mines remain in the ground because they are hard to detect and remove. The International Committee of the Red Cross estimated that in 2019 close to 110 million land mines were scattered across seventy countries. An estimated fifteen thousand to twenty thousand people are killed or injured by land mines each year. And the ongoing danger to people is why it is so important that these old land mines be removed.

Land mines are often in areas commonly used by local people.

How to Train Your HeroRAT

It takes about nine months for an African giant pouched rat to become a HeroRAT. Here's how they are trained:

STEP 1

When a pup is four weeks old and its eyes have opened, trainers begin handling and feeding it. This gets the rats used to people. The pup is introduced to different smells, such as soil, grass, and cooked food. It's also taken for rides in a truck—the way it will travel to work sites.

STEP 2

A six-week-old rat is trained to perform tasks that earn it a *click* from a clicker, and then it gets a food treat, such as a piece of banana. Bart said, "We discovered the rats will do anything to get those treats."

STEP 3

Once a young rat has learned a *click* means a reward, the rat is trained to work for that treat by finding a target scent—TNT. Trainers put stainless steel balls full of holes and containing TNT (chemically changed so the balls won't explode) on top of dirt. When a rat goes to one of those balls and sniffs it for at least five seconds, the trainer signals with a *click* and gives the rat its treat.

Next, balls with TNT are scattered among balls without TNT. The rat must find and sniff only the balls containing TNT to earn a *click* and a treat.

STEP 4

In the next training step, all the balls are buried in the dirt at marked locations. Now the rat must sniff out only the balls with TNT and scratch the dirt at those spots to earn a *click* and a treat.

STEP 5

Field training follows. The rat is taken to a 69-acre (28 ha) field containing more than a thousand land mines of several different types—all have been disabled so they can't explode. The field is divided into sections, each covering 1,076 square feet (100 sq. m). Some of these sections do not contain land mines. Others contain from one to four land mines. The locations of the land mines are marked with X and Y coordinates so the trainers know where they are.

The rat wears a nylon harness connected to a cord with two ends and a trainer at either end. These trainers gently direct the rat to move in lanes down the length of the field. When the rat correctly identifies the location of a buried land mine, it's rewarded with a *click* signaling it can come to the handler to receive a treat.

FINAL TEST

Trainee rats work through the pretend minefield five days a week, searching one or two sections a day. Once they regularly succeed at finding land mines, they face the final test—a blind test. This time, even the trainers don't know where the defused land mines are buried. To pass this test, the rat must locate the land mines with no more than two false alerts (signaling where no land mine exists). Any trainee that passes this test becomes a HeroRAT. From pup to HeroRAT takes around nine months of training. Bart said, "It still takes a person with a metal detector to get the mine's precise location and dig it up, but HeroRATs save time—save lives.

/// THE REST OF THE STORY

As of April 2020, APOPO was caring for fifty-three African giant poached rats that were working to detect land mines. Each year only a small number of HeroRATs are actively on the job. Yet from 2000 to 2020, HeroRATs are credited with locating more than 108,000 unexploded land mines and bombs for removal. As a result of their work, once-dangerous areas became available for farming and villagers were able to use roads safely that once crossed minefields. The HeroRATs are truly heroes.

A trained HeroRAT can check an area about the size of a tennis court for land mines in as little as twenty minutes. A person operating equipment to sweep for mines would need from one to four days to safely check the same area.

More Than Duty

June 8, 2015
Brewster, New York

BREWSTER,
NEW YORK

FROM GUIDE DOG TO BODYGUARD

One June day in 2015, Audrey Stone and her guide dog Figo (pronounced FEE-go), after the soccer star Luís Figo, were on their way home from their daily walk into town. Having very limited vision, Audrey counted on Figo to guide her everywhere—a job the dog had done successfully for six years. But Figo was about to go above and beyond the call of duty to keep Audrey safe.

Audrey Stone's guide dog was a gift from her local Lion's Club in 2009.

Audrey doesn't remember what happened next. However, those who were close enough to watch will never forget. As Audrey and Figo began crossing the street, the Brewster School's mini–school bus rounded the corner and drove straight at the pair. Witnesses said it was as if the bus driver didn't see Audrey, but Figo definitely saw the bus. He broke away from Audrey and dashed between her and the bus. At the last minute, Figo even leapt and bit the closest bus tire. The bus slammed to a stop as it struck Figo!

People rushed to help Audrey and lift Figo from under the bus.

After the accident, the ribbons Audrey had tied on Figo's harness that morning became decorations for a hero.

Audrey was knocked down hard. Though she was injured, the bus had stopped just in time to keep from running over her. Figo had saved her life.

People rushed to help Audrey, and with the local fire station just across the street, the firefighters were there within minutes. Figo's leg was bleeding, and he couldn't stand on it. One firefighter wrapped Figo's injured leg to protect it until a veterinarian could treat it. Even though he was hurt, Figo remained totally focused on Audrey as the first responders tended to her. Audrey said, "Figo dragged himself over to me. He wanted to make sure I was OK. I believe he'd been ready to die for me. That's what tore me apart."

Once the ambulance arrived, Audrey was rushed to Danbury Hospital. She had a broken ankle, broken ribs, a fractured elbow, and a head wound. A police officer took Figo to the Middlebranch Veterinary clinic.

Figo went for his monthlong retraining program at the Guide Dog Foundation in Smithtown, Long Island, New York, where he was originally trained.

/// CAN FIGO RETURN TO WORK?

Figo's leg was broken, and his veterinarian LouAnn Pfeifer operated to set it. Then he remained at the clinic for a little over three months, while waiting for the broken bone to fully heal. Figo continued to need care while Audrey was in the hospital and later a facility that helped her learn to walk again.

By the time both had recovered, Audrey worried Figo might not be able to be her guide dog anymore. He was, after all, eight years old. And when a guide dog hasn't been working for an extended period, it might switch to pet mode and refuse to be a guide. But Audrey was hopeful. So that fall Figo went for a refresher guide dog training course. Audrey said, "Before he left, I told Figo, 'You're going back to school to retrain and you're going to do it. Then you're coming back to me.'"

And Figo did.

Audrey and Figo were very happy to be together again.

/// THE REST OF THE STORY

The day of the accident, the story of Figo's heroism went global on social media and then appeared on television and in newspapers. A flood of flowers and letters with praise for Figo and concern for both Audrey and Figo arrived at the hospital while she was there. Audrey was even interviewed from her hospital room on the *Today Show* and *Good Morning America*.

After so much news coverage, the world wanted to know the end of the story. A crowd of reporters was there when Figo returned to Audrey to resume his guide dog duties. More important to Audrey was that LouAnn Pfeifer, most of Audrey's neighbors, and the firefighters from across the street were there too. The pair's reunion didn't disappoint.

Figo climbed out of the car and, at his first glimpse of Audrey, started wagging his tail nonstop. When he reached Audrey, she leaned down to give Figo a welcome-home hug. Audrey said, "I feel there had to be something in the universe that gave me Figo, because when I needed him, he took charge." And now they were a pair again.

Audrey and Figo left their friends and all the reporters behind to take their first walk together since the accident.

Figo was also honored for his bravery during the ASPCA's Annual Humane Awards Luncheon in New York City.

That November, Figo was awarded the 2015 American Society for the Prevention of Cruelty to Animals Dog of the Year Award. While Audrey was very proud of Figo for receiving that honor, it mattered most to her that she had her best friend back again. And he continued to guide her. In 2019 Audrey reported, "Even at 11 years old, Figo's doing very well. So am I. We're definitely better together."

Search and Rescue Heroes

HUNTER'S STORY

January 15, 2010
Port-au-Prince, Haiti

Disaster hit Haiti on January 12, 2010, when a 7.0-magnitude earthquake struck the island. A large part of the capital city, Port-au-Prince, was reduced to rubble. William (Billy) Monahan and his search and rescue dog, Hunter, from the Los Angeles County Fire Department in Palmdale, California, were part of the team of six dogs and handlers sent to help by the National Disaster Search Dog Foundation. By the time they arrived three days later on January 15, the time window for having the best chance of rescuing survivors was almost up. It is generally believed the longest a trapped, injured person can stay alive without water, food, and medical care is seventy-two hours. The city was divided into search zones, and Billy and Hunter went straight to their assigned zone. They started searching among the chunks of concrete, smashed glass, and tangled metal.

PORT-AU-PRINCE, HAITI

Hunter, an eight-year-old border collie, was trained as part of the Urban Search and Rescue team from Fire Station 136 of the Los Angeles County Fire Department.

The day was hot, and the conditions were rugged. Still, even as the day wore on and no search proved successful, Billy and Hunter kept going. Then, while crossing the remains of a collapsed four-story apartment building, Hunter leapt ahead. When he stopped, he gave the signal: *Bark! Bark! Bark!* That was how he'd been trained to show he'd found someone alive.

All at once, Hunter went from picking his way slowly to bounding as though tracking a scent.

The young woman survivor was trapped when the four floors of her apartment house pancaked down.

Billy and other members of his rescue team hurried over to Hunter. Billy called, "Is anyone in there?" Hearing a faint sound that might have been someone answering, Billy took his water bottle and secured it to a stick he plucked out of the wreckage. He lowered the bottle through a crack in the concrete rubble where he thought he'd heard a voice.

In 2011 Hunter was honored with the American Kennel Club's Humane Fund Award for Canine Excellence in the Search and Rescue Dog category.

Seconds later, he felt a tug and pulled up the stick without the water bottle.

Hunter had done it! He'd found someone to rescue.

Other search and rescue teams joined them. They used concrete saws and jackhammers to clear debris. They also crawled into narrow openings and hauled out rubble in buckets. Little by little, the rescuers got closer to the survivor. Finally, after nearly twenty hours, they pulled out the trapped woman who had called out from the ruins. In fact, there were three women survivors close together who were saved.

Billy and Hunter continued searching other sites, searching for hope and finding it. For sixteen days, they worked with the other dog and handler search teams from the National Disaster Search Dog Foundation. During that time, Billy and Hunter helped rescue twelve survivors.

Born in 2002, Hunter's search and rescue training began in 2004. He trained for two years before starting search and rescue work, and he kept training and going on missions until his retirement in January 2018 at the incredible age of fifteen.

FOR THE JOB TRAINING

Dogs make ideal search and rescue animals. In addition to their keen sense of smell, they can go into smaller, less stable places than people can safely search. For the dogs, search and rescue training starts out as play. Each dog has one special toy, and during each training session that toy is hidden. So the dog must find its toy to have a chance to play. In later training sessions, the dog must find a hidden person who has its toy to have a chance to play.

To become a certified US Federal Emergency Management Agency (FEMA) search and rescue dog, dogs must pass a final test. This includes climbing a ladder, walking a plank that's off the ground, and finding two people—at least one buried in rubble and invisible to both the dog and the dog's handler. Then, as will happen during real search missions, the handler takes out the dog's toy and briefly engages in playtime. That's the reward the dog works for. But the dog's rescue effort can save lives.

CHILI'S STORY

January 2017
Austrian Alps, Austria

Snow swirled in the wind, stirred by a landing helicopter. The helicopter door was already open, so Sepp Bucher and his golden retriever, Chili, launched onto the snowfield ahead of the rest of the search and rescue team. They were there from Austria's Internationale Rettungshunde Organisation (International Rescue Dog Organization) to help because there wouldn't be a rescue unless Chili could locate the skier who'd been buried by the avalanche on the Austrian mountain that January day.

AUSTRIAN ALPS, AUSTRIA

This is an avalanche—a sudden movement of a mass of snow, ice, and rocks down a mountainside. This avalanche happened in Austria.

In perfect conditions, with dry, fluffy snow, an avalanche rescue dog's keen nose is able to pick up scents as far as 20 feet (6 m) below the surface.

The buried skier wasn't wearing an avalanche beacon (a device that gives off a pulsed radio signal that a receiver can pick up). However, when Sepp received the call on his cell phone reporting the avalanche, he was only 12 miles (19 km) away, cross-country skiing with his search and rescue dog, Chili. There was already a helicopter on its way to the site, and it quickly stopped to pick up Sepp and Chili. This timing was critical, because a person buried under a load of snow has the best chance of surviving if rescued during the first twenty minutes. Chili was on-site with her nose to the snow, sniffing and searching, just five minutes after the call.

Chili had only been searching for two minutes when she started barking and digging so frantically that snow pelted Sepp as he held onto her leash.

The team trusted Chili's cue and went to work, using probes (poles with measurements along the shaft) to let them know how deep to dig.

Next, the search and rescue team hauled out shovels and started digging. Before joining in, Sepp pulled Chili's toy out of his coat pocket and played tug-of-war with her briefly as her reward. She needed that reinforcement every time—on real missions as well as during training—to perform well as a search and rescue dog. Then, while Chili watched, Sepp and the rescue team attacked the snow. First, they dug. Then, dropping to their knees, they scooped and scraped away more snow and ice.

The search and rescue team pulled the skier to safety.

Woof! Chili gave a doggie cheer as Sepp and the others lifted the survivor out of the snow and carried him to the waiting helicopter. Moments later, with everyone on board, the helicopter was in the air and headed to the nearest hospital. Thanks to Chili's keen sense of smell and training, the search and rescue team gave this avalanche rescue a happy ending.

Note: The photos accompanying the avalanche rescue are not of the actual event because when time is critical, and a life is at stake, there isn't time to take pictures.

GUARDING PENGUINS

September 2005
Middle Island, Warrnambool
Coast, Australia

WARRNAMBOOL, AUSTRALIA

PENGUIN PROBLEMS

In the spring of 2005, the residents of Warrnambool (pronounced WAR-nam-bool) on the coast of southwestern Victoria, Australia, were shocked to discover fewer than ten adult little penguins nesting on Middle Island. Before 2005 as many as eight hundred little penguins had been counted on the island. That rocky bit of land in Stingray Bay was not far offshore from the city. It was a wildlife sanctuary and home to a breeding colony of little penguins, the world's smallest penguin species.

Male and female little penguins look alike except the male's beak is often broader.

Little penguins have been raising their chicks on Middle Island for so long that their feet have worn paths in the island's sandstone between the gravel beach and their nesting areas.

No other animals lived on the island with the penguin colony. However, at low tide, predators, such as foxes, could walk across the exposed sandy clay and easily reach the wildlife sanctuary to hunt the penguins. Because of these predators, the little penguin colony had gotten smaller and smaller over the years. In 2005 the population hit that dramatic low. If the breeding colony was to have a chance of surviving and to increase in size again, something had to be done. The question was, What could be done?

Ian Fitzgibbon, former manager of the Warrnambool City Council, said, "There were so many foxes and getting across to Middle Island was so easy. We didn't know how to protect the remaining penguins from these hunters."

That was, until a local farmer, Allan "Swampy" Marsh, had an idea.

IT'S A LITTLE PENGUIN'S LIFE

Little penguins are just 13 inches (33 cm) tall and weigh only about 2.2 pounds (1 kg). They spend most of their lives in the ocean feeding on squid and small fish, such as anchovies. But once a year, October through March, the adults come ashore to form colonies (groups) along the coasts of Australia and New Zealand. Then mating pairs scratch out nesting burrows where they lay their eggs and raise their chicks.

For the first three to four weeks after the chicks hatch, the parents take turns guarding the nest burrow and going to sea to feed. On its return, the feeding parent brings up food from its stomach for the growing chicks to eat. For another four weeks, both parents go to sea during the day to catch food for themselves and to bring home food to the chicks. They return at sunset and stay in the burrow, guarding the chicks overnight.

By February the chicks are young adults. They've exchanged their downy coat for waterproof feathers and are ready to go to sea and hunt for their own food.

The female lays two eggs, and the pair shares the job of incubating them for about thirty-five days until the chicks hatch.

/// GUARDIAN ANGEL DOGS

On his farm, Swampy had Maremmas: big, shaggy sheepdogs. They weren't good at herding, but they were great natural guardians. These dogs were willing to protect the animals they accepted as their responsibility by barking loudly and scaring away anything that came too close. Swampy used Maremmas to guard his chickens from foxes, so he figured the dogs could do the job of protecting the little penguins.

The Middle Island Maremma Project was started by the Warrnambool City Council in 2006 to have Maremma dogs guard the little penguin colony. One of Swampy's dogs was the first guardian of the colony. The penguin research team from Australia's Deakin University was eager to see if the dog kept the foxes away and how it behaved with the little penguins. After a couple of weeks, all seemed to be going well. So the training program, led by dog handler David Williams, began for the dogs to become official penguin guardians.

Nighttime is the most important time for the dog guardians to be on duty because that's when most predators attack. So, over time, the dogs became mostly active at night and slept during the daytime.

The chosen trainees were two Maremma pups. The training was a highly supervised, six-month program. The goals were to get the dogs used to being on Middle Island while they were young and used to being around the little penguins. As the Maremmas learned to accept the little penguins as their responsibility, the little penguins also learned to trust the dogs. But would the dogs being on Middle Island keep the little penguins safe from the foxes?

The dogs were more guarding the island from things not usually there than specifically watching over the penguins. So, other birds, such as cormorants and oystercatchers, were also protected by the dogs.

During the breeding season, a pair of guardian dogs took turns working five to six days a week on Middle Island. They watched out for the penguins by patrolling a wooden deck where the dogs were provided with food and water. As hoped, just the dogs being near the breeding colony proved enough to keep the foxes away. Researcher Anne Wallis who worked on studying the Middle Island little penguin colony said, "By the 2012[–]2013 [breeding season] September count, there were 103 adults."

By 2016 the number of little penguins coming ashore to breed had grown to 123 adults, and recovery was looking good. Then, in 2017, a period of extremely high tides and bad weather made it impossible to take the dogs over to Middle Island for a long time. Before the guardian dogs were returned to duty, foxes managed to reach the wildlife sanctuary and kill 70 adult little penguins. During the next year—the 2018–2019 breeding season—only 50 adult little penguins came ashore on Middle Island. However, that year breeding activity produced ten new chicks, a higher than expected number. It gave the members of the Middle Island Maremma Project hope.

/// THE REST OF THE STORY

What happened in 2017 proved the importance of having the guardian dogs watching over the little penguin colony. Since then the trained Maremmas have been on duty patrolling Middle Island the entire time during each little penguin breeding season. With their help, the little penguin population will hopefully continue to increase.

During the off-season, the guardian dogs stay on a farm near Warrnambool. New guardian puppies continue to be trained, so replacement guardian dogs will always be ready to take over. Eudy and Tula, named after the little penguin's scientific name *Eudyptula minor*, were the sixth and seventh guardian dogs. Tula retired in 2019, while Eudy continued working on the island watching over new puppies as they were training. The next two dogs to assume guardianship are Mezzo and Isola. The protection of the little penguin breeding colony is in their paws. Eudy will retire soon, and another Maremma puppy is already in training for the future.

Maremmas usually only work until they are six or seven years old, so new pups are regularly in training to become future penguin guardians.

Bring in the Elephants

December 26, 2004
Banda Aceh, Indonesia

BANDA ACEH, INDONESIA

DISASTER!

On December 26, 2004, a 9.1-magnitude earthquake struck parts of Indonesia. One of the most powerful earthquakes ever recorded, it caused the ocean floor off the coast of northern Sumatra to suddenly rise 130 feet (40 m). That triggered a tsunami, a large ocean wave caused by sudden movement of the ocean floor. A tsunami moves across the open ocean with great speed, and in shallow water near the shore, it builds into a giant, powerful wave. Off Sumatra, a tsunami rolled toward land at 500 miles (800 km) per hour. When it hit, Banda Aceh (pronounced BAND-uh AH-chaa) was struck with incredible force.

Within twenty minutes of the undersea earthquake, 100-foot-high (30 m) waves slammed ashore at Banda Aceh.

Surging water ripped out trees and demolished buildings along the beach. Then the wave plowed into the city, shoving a mountain of debris ahead of it. The impact was devastating!

By the time the water slid back to the shore, much of Banda Aceh was smashed or buried under rubble. Thousands of people were dead or missing—many more were homeless and had lost everything. But no working equipment was available to search for people or salvage anything useful. And it would likely be many days before rescue equipment could be shipped or flown in. However, just a short distance away in the tropical rain forest, there was help—eight Sumatran elephants.

Washed-out bridges, mud-buried roads, and a damaged port and airport all slowed relief efforts from reaching Banda Aceh.

Elephants did the work of trucks and bulldozers.

Normally, the elephants lived at a camp about 31 miles (50 km) south of Banda Aceh. There, they carried government forest rangers through the rain forest to patrol for illegal loggers and poachers trying to catch endangered tigers and rhinos. But those rangers had homes and families in Banda Aceh. When word of the disaster reached them, they loaded the elephants into trucks to transport them quickly to Banda Aceh. Once they got close, the road became blocked, so they unloaded the elephants. From there, mahouts, the elephant handlers, rode the elephants the rest of the way. They arrived in Banda Aceh five days after the tsunami struck and immediately went to work, guiding the elephants to help their own families and the community. The elephants cleared the roads of fallen trees and debris. They lifted and moved twisted metal and broken concrete so whatever wasn't destroyed could be recovered.

News of the elephants being taken to Banda Aceh reached Christopher Stremme, a German wildlife veterinarian working in Indonesia with the Veterinary Society for Sumatran Wildlife Conservation. His job was to provide health checkups and treatments to captive elephants in Indonesia, and he knew the elephants at Banda Aceh would need care. So, about five days after the elephants arrived (ten days after the tsunami), Christopher and his team reached Banda Aceh. He found the elephants where they spent their nights in an abandoned parking lot.

He said, "It was a very difficult work area for the elephants because they were walking on debris with glass, iron nails, chunks of concrete, or whatever else." Besides having some injuries, Christopher found the animals were in poor condition after working for almost a week without sufficient food and water. After all, there was very little for the people either. But Christopher knew, if the elephants were to keep helping, he needed to improve things for them.

Christopher Stremme is a wildlife veterinarian who specializes in caring for elephants.

The elephants moved wrecked cars, motorcycles, and other rubbish.

Christopher immediately went to work treating any cuts and wounds on the elephants. His team also took over supplying food and water for the elephants. They hired a truck, and every morning after the elephants headed off to work, they drove inland from Banda Aceh on any passable roads to reach villages unaffected by the tsunami. There, they collected coconut palm leaves, banana tree leaves, and sugarcane to feed the elephants. They also filled as many water barrels as they could carry for the elephants.

Meanwhile, the elephants continued working. Their job was important—helping the survivors salvage anything that would help them stay alive.

Every day Christopher carefully checked each elephant and treated any cuts, scrapes, or other injuries.

/// THE REST OF THE STORY

For about two and a half months following the tsunami, the elephants stayed in Banda Aceh to help. Along the coast, entire villages were flattened, leaving all the survivors homeless. So the toppled coconut trees the elephants collected became building materials to create temporary housing. The whole time the elephants were there working, Christopher and his team stayed there too, caring for the elephants.

Finally, the elephants were trucked back to the rain forest, and they went back to carrying rangers on patrols, guarding the area's trees and wildlife. And Christopher went back to work helping captive elephants stay healthy and promoting wild elephant conservation efforts.

The elephants loaded boards onto trucks so whatever was usable could add to the supply of building materials.

49

TARA THE TERRIFIC!

May 13, 2014
Bakersfield, California

WATCH OUT!

It was a warm, sunny afternoon in May, and four-year-old Jeremy Triantafilo was riding his bike in front of his home. Near the house, Jeremy's mother, Erica, was pulling out the weeds that were trying to take over a flower bed. And comfortably curled under a bush nearby was Tara, the family cat. Then the neighbor's driveway gate opened.

Out dashed the neighbor's dog, a stocky Labrador-chow mix. It shot across the driveway and into Jeremy. *CRASH!* Boy and bike went over and down. The dog growled. Jeremy howled!

TO THE RESCUE

In a flash, Tara charged in, attacking the dog with teeth and claws. The dog fled with Tara on its heels, making sure it kept going all the

Tara was a stray that followed Roger and Erica home one night after a neighborhood soccer game.

This scene, captured by the family's security camera, showed Tara dashing to Jeremy's defense.

way to its own family's yard. Jeremy's mother looked up to see the dog leaving and her son was bleeding. She rushed him to the doctor. Luckily, Jeremy just had scrapes and bruises.

It was only later, that evening, when the family was safely back home that Erica and Jeremy's father, Roger, checked their home security camera's footage from that afternoon. They were surprised to discover that Tara had chased the dog away from their son. Roger said, "Till then, we'd always thought of Tara as being the lucky one because we adopted her. Now we knew we were the lucky ones because she adopted us."

The Triantafilo family today: parents, Erica and Roger; Jeremy; and, of course, Tara.

/// THE REST OF THE STORY

Jeremy said, "Tara's a hero!" When the YouTube video of Tara rescuing Jeremy went viral, people around the world agreed. On June 19, 2015, Tara officially became a hero. The Society for the Prevention of Cruelty to Animals (SPCA) in Los Angeles altered their annual award for the most heroic dog to most heroic cat just to honor Tara.

Ever alert, Tara checks out her award.

NEVER-ENDING
STORIES

//

Some animals are trained to save human lives in dangerous times or risky places. Other times an animal's instinct or natural behavior kicks in. Then a rescue happens, because that animal was in the right place at the right time. Sometimes, it's enough that an animal is there, offering its support. The stories of animals being heroic are never-ending . . . and wonderful! That's something to be grateful for in a world full of challenges.

On November 4, 2016, this little girl is comforted by her dog amid the ruins of her home following fires that destroyed 280 homes in Cantagallo, Peru.

A Note from Sandra Markle

I admit it—I *love* animals. I also respect what animals can do and what amazing selfless acts they are capable of accomplishing. So, writing this book was a dream job for me. It gave me the opportunity to interview people about their experiences training and working with assistance or rescue animals. Best of all, this book motivated me to track down those special survivors who have had their lives saved by animals. Listening to their awestruck stories of what happened and how they were rescued was amazing.

I'm delighted to share these stories with you, especially the stories of some special animals who have rescued other animals. And I love the stories where an animal's instinctive, or natural, behavior made all the difference in someone's quality of life. After all, making someone's life better is heroic.

Glossary

avalanche: the sudden movement of a mass of snow, ice, and rocks down a mountainside

earthquake: a sudden, violent shaking of the ground due to a movement within Earth's crust or volcanic activity

guide dog: a dog trained to help someone with a disability

instinct: a pattern of behavior that a person or animal is born with

minefield: an area planted with explosive mines

nesting area: a place where a group of animals gather to mate and raise their young

orphan: a young animal or person without parents

poacher: a person who hunts or catches animals illegally

search and rescue dog: a dog trained to find missing people or people trapped by accident or disaster

tsunami: a long, high, powerful ocean wave caused by an earthquake or undersea landslide

Source Notes

7   Nan Hauser, interview with the author, November 13, 2018.

9   Hauser.

9   Hauser.

11   Lente Roode, interview with the author, December 30, 2019.

11   Roode.

13   Roode.

17   Bart Weetjens, interview with the author, December 15, 2017.

20   Weetjens.

23   Weetjens.

28   Audrey Stone, interview with the author, November 27, 2018.

29   Stone.

30   Stone.

30   Stone.

33   William Monahan, interview with the author, January 21, 2019.

39   Ian Fitzgibbon, interview with the author, December 16, 2014.

42   Anne Wallis, interview with the author, January 5, 2020.

47   Christopher Stremme, interview with the author, January 5, 2020.

51   Roger Triantafilo, interview with the author, September 15, 2019.

51   Triantafilo.

Dig Deeper

To find out even more, check out the following books and websites:

Books

Boothroyd, Jennifer. *Hero Service Dogs*. Minneapolis: Lerner Publications, 2017. Find out what service dogs do and how they help save lives.

Claybourne, Anna. *Humpback Whales*. Chicago: Heinemann, 2013. Dynamite photos and fun facts combine to share the lives and behavior of these ocean giants.

Hurt, Avery. *Elephants*. Washington, DC: National Geographic, 2016. Learn all about different kinds of elephants, their lives, and their behavior.

Squire, Ann O. *Tsunamis*. New York: Children's Press, 2016. Readers learn about some of the world's tsunamis and why they caused so much damage.

Websites

About Animals: Sumatran Elephant
https://www.aboutanimals.com/mammal/sumatran-elephant/
Explore the Sumatran elephant—the kind of elephant that helped the survivors of the Banda Aceh tsunami.

Penguin World: Little Penguin
http://www.penguinworld.com/types/little.html
Learn more about Australia's little penguins.

See Tara Come to the Rescue
https://www.youtube.com/watch?v=LSG_wBiTEE8
Watch the real-life rescue.

Watch Lammie and Little G
https://www.youtube.com/watch?v=0bL02GyIsKw
See Lammie and Little G romping and playing together.

INDEX

PHOTO ACKNOWLEDGMENTS

Image credits: Stephen J. Boitano/Getty Images, pp. 1, 47; NICHOLAS KAMM/Getty Images, pp. 1, 5; MARK RALSTON/AFP/Getty Images, pp. 1, 51; © Lawinenhundestaffel Salzburg, Austria, pp. 1, 36; VW Pics/Getty Images, pp. 1, 7; Courtesy of the Middle Island Penguin Project (www.warrnamboolpenguins.com.au), pp. 1, 42, 43; Laura Westlund/Independent Picture Service, pp. 2–3, 6, 10, 16, 25, 31, 35, 38, 44, 50; Dave Kotinsky/Getty Images, p. 6 (top); Education Images/Getty Images, p. 6 (bottom); © Caters News, p. 8; Andrey Nekrasov/Barcroft Media/Getty Images, p. 9; © Richard Du Toit /Minden Pictures, p. 10; © Courtesy of HESC, pp. 11 (left, right), 12 (left, right), 14; Martin Harvey/Getty Images, p. 13; Gail Shotlander/Getty Images, p. 15; Xavier ROSSI/Gamma-Rapho/Getty Images, pp. 16, 17, 21 (top, bottom), 24; APOPO, pp. 18, 20 (top); Ulrich Baumgarten/Getty Images, p. 19; AP Photo/Denis Gray, pp. 20 (bottom), 22; CARL DE SOUZA/AFP/Getty Images, p. 23; AP Photo/Seth Wenig, pp. 25, 28, 29; © Frank Becerra/Brewster Fire Department, pp. 26, 27; Daniel Zuchnik/WireImage/Getty Images, p. 30; Courtesy of William Monahan, pp. 31, 32, 33, 34; U.S. Navy/Getty Images, p. 32; AP Photo/RUDI BLAHA, p. 35; RAYMOND ROIG/AFP/Getty Images, p. 37; Auscape International Pty Ltd/Alamy Stock Photo, p. 38; phototrip/Alamy Stock Photo, p. 39; Doug Gimesy/naturepl.com, p. 40; Liam Driver/Newspix/Getty Images, p. 41; JOHN RUSSELL/AFP/Getty Images, p. 44; AFP/Getty Images, p. 45; Suzanne Plunkett/Photographer, p. 46; © Christopher Stremme, p. 47; ROMEO GACAD/AFP/Getty Images, p. 48; © Roger Triantafilo, p. 50; Courtesy of Roger Triantafilo, p. 51; AP Photo/Richard Vogel, p. 51; Sebastian Castaneda/Anadolu Agency/Getty Images, p. 53.

Cover image: Stephen J. Boitano/Getty Images.